NATIVE
Foreigner

NATIVE
Foreigner

by

BEVERLY P. GORDON

XULON PRESS

Xulon Press
555 Winderley Pl, Suite 225
Maitland, FL 32751
407.339.4217
www.xulonpress.com

© 2024 by Beverly P. Gordon

All rights reserved solely by the author. The author guarantees all contents are original and do not infringe upon the legal rights of any other person or work. No part of this book may be reproduced in any form without the permission of the author.

Due to the changing nature of the Internet, if there are any web addresses, links, or URLs included in this manuscript, these may have been altered and may no longer be accessible. The views and opinions shared in this book belong solely to the author and do not necessarily reflect those of the publisher. The publisher therefore disclaims responsibility for the views or opinions expressed within the work.

Paperback ISBN-13: 978-1-66289-554-8
Ebook ISBN-13: 978-1-66289-555-5

CONTENTS

Author's Notes..................................... ix

Introduction xv

Chapter One   **The Psychology of Acculturation**
*Theoretical framework for understanding
acculturation* 1

Chapter Two   **Migration Experiences**
*An autobiographical case study of the
author's migration experiences* 5

Chapter Three **Jamaican Migration History**
*Historical events that explain Jamaican
culture and migration experience* 17

Chapter Four   **Jamaican Voices**
*Qualitative reports from Jamaicans living
in Northeastern USA. Data received from
recorded structured interviews* 27

Chapter Five   **Finding the Way Home**
*Spiritual perspective on migration and
acculturation* 47

Chapter Six   **Homecoming**
Reflections on a visit to Jamaica 63

Author's Notes

My personality development has been significantly influenced by my experiences of migration. I write from the perspective of one who is fundamentally Jamaican in speech and ideology yet acutely aware of missing elements in the fabric of my cultural internal environment that is a result of many years spent in "foreign" lands. My perspective, though deeply patriotic, is a fusion of the various cultural contexts in which I have resided.

The purpose of this book is not only to document the experiences of Jamaican immigrants to the United States, but to provide a socio-cultural lens for perceiving and interpreting the behaviors of individuals who have migrated from the Caribbean region, particularly Jamaica. It is also my purpose to emphasize the power of Christian faith to build resilience and coping skills for Christian immigrants.

Migration is a common part of Jamaican life. It is common practice for families to migrate to other countries from Jamaica. Most Jamaican migration is to England, Canada, and the United States, but Jamaicans can be found residing in most countries around the world. Even though Jamaican migration is largely voluntary, acculturative stress is still experienced among this group of immigrants.

Don't Ask Me Why

I'm tired of defending myself, my ethnicity, my people, and the size of my country.

I'm tired of giving a reason for being here. Why are you here?

I'm tired of being a foreigner, an outsider, the one with the accent.

I'm here because I want to be. You act as if it's all yours and I have no right to it, but it's not yours and it's not mine.

My ancestors helped to build this that you hold so dear and so selfishly.

It's as much mine as it is yours, if indeed it belongs to either of us.

Don't ask me why I'm here. I'm here because I want to be.

Living in the present is good; but at some point, we need to come to peace with the past so that we can use it in combination with present reality to make the best decisions for the future. Avoidance of past realities detracts from our wise use of physical, mental, and spiritual resources in the present and future.

Sometimes in the press of life we forget our original dreams and goals. Every now and then we need to go back to where we started to regain perspective and press on to achieve our dreams. Sometimes looking back gives power to our dreams and energy to our endeavors.

Introduction

Immigrants to the United States of America are confronted with the task of adjusting to a society that is complex and very diverse in nature. This fact alone places the immigrant at risk for developing adjustment-related changes in behavior. Many studies have documented the experiences of Hispanic, European, and Asian groups, but relatively sparse research exists that addresses the acculturation patterns and psychological adjustments of Black immigrants from Africa and the Caribbean.

Native Foreigner examines first-hand accounts from a small sample of Jamaicans living in the United States and describes psychological experiences and adjustments in four areas: acculturation, ethnic identity, well-being, and spirituality. Jamaican migration experience is examined against the backdrop of the author's own migration experiences and that of seven other Christian Jamaican immigrants to the United States.

Christian ideology and worldview embrace the belief in unity and inclusivity. The Jamaican immigrant who is also a committed Christian faces another layer of adjustment that can have a life-changing impact. The idea of separate worship communities for different races and ethnicities is foreign to the concept of Christianity for the Jamaican Christian. The Jamaican national motto, "Out of Many One People," takes on a deeper meaning for the Christian Jamaican who, before migration, conceptualized the church as a world-wide family of believers. *Native Foreigner* dares to openly confront the issue of race within the church and the psychological impact on immigrants.

Spirituality is deeply ingrained in the mentality of Jamaicans. The challenge of acculturation for Christian Jamaican immigrants is intensified by the practice of racial segregation within the church.

Despite the secular and religious challenges, Jamaican immigrants respond with resilience and hope as they adjust and flourish in a system that is not designed to facilitate their success. Family and church community continue to be effective sources of social support for Jamaican immigrants. Whether they belong to an organized religious body or simply practice a lifestyle that is guided by spiritual values, spirituality and social support have been reported as strong factors in the development of resilience and adaptation among Jamaican immigrants.

The immigrant's restless longing for a spiritual refuge from the inequities and injustices of earthly systems is denied fulfillment even in the church. There seems to be no balm for the wounded souls of people who have been uprooted from their earthly homes, voluntarily or involuntarily, and the wound is deepened with each day spent as native foreigners in their homeland, in their adopted country of citizenship, and even in their church. Despite exclusion, division, and segregation, they find sanctuary in the familiarity of beliefs, practices, and traditions that remind them of home. These native foreigners seek a place of emotional refuge. In absence of this fulfillment, the native foreigner clings passionately to their memories of "home."

Chapter One

The Psychology of Acculturation: A Theoretical Framework

John W. Berry's seminal theory of acculturation forms the theoretical framework for this book. According to this theory, immigrants choose one or more paths of adjustment when faced with new cultural norms. These choices result in patterns of behavior that influence development, psychological processes, and behavior.

Berry proposed a model of acculturation that categorizes individual adaptation strategies between two dimensions. The first dimension concerns the retention or rejection of an individual's native culture (i.e., "Is it considered to be of value to maintain one's identity and characteristics?"). The second dimension concerns the adoption or rejection of the host culture ("Is it considered to be of value to maintain relationships with the larger society?"). From these two questions, four acculturation strategies emerge:

- Assimilation occurs when individuals adopt the cultural norms of a dominant or host culture, over their original culture.
- Separation occurs when individuals reject the dominant or host culture in favor of preserving their culture of origin. Separation is often facilitated by immigration to ethnic enclaves.
- Integration occurs when individuals can adopt the cultural norms of the dominant or host culture while maintaining their culture of origin. Integration leads to and is often synonymous with biculturalism.
- Marginalization occurs when individuals reject both their culture of origin and the dominant host culture (Worthy, et al., 2022).

Culture is recognized as a significant force in determining individual behavior. When individuals live in environments where new cultural norms are introduced, as in migration, the person is impacted and challenged to make cognitive and behavioral adjustments.

Cross-cultural psychology has demonstrated important links between cultural context and individual behavioral development. Given this relationship, cross-cultural research has increasingly investigated what happens to individuals who have developed in one cultural context when they attempt to re-establish their lives in another one. The long-term psychological consequences of this process of acculturation are highly variable, depending on social and personal variables that reside in the society of origin, the society of settlement. and phenomena that both exist prior to, and arise during, the course of acculturation (Berry, 1997).

Assimilation is difficult for Black immigrants in America. Assimilation for Jamaican immigrants is particularly difficult because of the multicultural and multiethnic nature of this group of people. Jamaican immigrants have been identified as one group of immigrants to the United States who experience tridimensional acculturation: orientation towards three cultures. Furthermore, triculturalism has been shown to have both negative and positive consequences. It has been associated with negative psychological adjustment; although, it has also been shown to provide positive contributions to adaptation and acculturation (Ferguson, et. al., 2014).

To adopt the cultural norms of the dominant culture, it would necessitate conformity to White norms and values. The Black Jamaican immigrant has a life history and cultural habits that more closely resemble that of Black Americans. However, the colonization of countries like Jamaica has left residual patterns of indoctrination that more closely resembles the thinking patterns and biases of White colonists. This unique mixture of native consciousness and internalized European values often result in misunderstandings between Black Americans and Caribbean immigrants. Hence, Jamaican immigrants occupy a distinct ethnic group that portrays the rich amalgamation of ethnic ideals that reflect the multicultural influences that have played significant roles in the development of Jamaican culture.

It is conceivable then that persons who have had multiple migration experiences at different times across the lifespan might experience more psychological distress even while having greater capacity for adjustment based on longer exposure to acculturation stress.

Chapter Two

Personal Migration Adjustments

On December 23, 1954, I was born to proud and happy Jamaican parents. There was no national fanfare. I was just another Jamaican baby like all the others born that day on our sunny island home. Sunshine kissed the wide-open Jamaican sky to welcome my birth. For the next ten years of my innocent, carefree life, I knew only the warmth of sunshine and the joy of my family's love. I was a happy child. Any fleeting moments of sadness were quickly absorbed by the sheer joy and beauty of my life. I was loved and cherished. I blossomed and grew.

The first turning point of my life was when my family migrated to live in London, England. As a part of the British Commonwealth, Jamaica had enjoyed the rich heritage of British culture. The acculturation process was somewhat facilitated by that colonial familiarity. Nevertheless, there was a process of adjustment. My ballpoint pen became a "biro." My coat was an "anorak." My hat that covered my head, neck, and part of my face was a "balaclava." "Tomaytoes" became "tomahtoes."

The most significant change for me was the realization that I was "colored." This was an amazing discovery that altered my perception of the world. Not only was I colored, but there was something innately wrong with being "colored." Prior to this life-changing revelation, I had regarded myself as an attractive, normal human being. Now, these facts were in question. But I was young and lighthearted and didn't allow it to spoil my fun too much.

My introduction to British elementary schooling was pleasant. I made several friends and had lots of fun. The only other "colored" person in my class was a girl named Helen. Truly, she wasn't "colored." She was a "half-caste" since one parent was White and the other Black.

It was during this first year at school in London that I experienced my one and only fight. A little girl sat behind me every day and took devilish delight in pulling my two pigtails while calling me "black bastard" and other unpleasant names. I ignored her and did my best to avoid her. On the fateful day, I was happily playing French skipping with my friends when Vera (not her real name) decided to escalate the taunting. She was determined to get my attention, even though I did my usual strategy of ignoring her. Something snapped inside of me when she engaged me physically by pushing me while still calling me names. My pent-up rage exploded in a volley of blows to the startled girl who fought back but was no match for my fury that day.

The worst part of that experience for me was when the headmaster reprimanded me harshly without asking for any details of the event, and then punished me with several biting strokes of his cane to my hands. The suppressed rage that I felt gave me the courage to utter no sound and shed no tear at what I perceived to be gross injustice.

Later, in high school when I was similarly provoked by a group of White students who thought it was clever to make derogatory remarks about my hair and my mother, I had matured enough to simply walk away. It helped to have my White friend put her arm around my shoulder and say sadly, "I'm so sorry that you're not White. I hate that you have to go through this." She meant well.

I did well academically as I always had. I soon absorbed the culture and became quite British in my thinking. My confidence did waver just a little bit when I was subjected to a placement test soon after my arrival in London. Since this was to be my final year of elementary education, I needed to be placed in a secondary school for the following school year, which would begin September 1966.

Based on my educational records from Jamaica and my initial performance at the primary school in Balham, London, I was slated for one of the more prestigious secondary schools. The placement test went well regarding all subjects except social studies. To my dismay, that test was based entirely on British and European current events and government processes and personalities. Had I been given a culturally relevant test in that subject; it is likely that I would have passed with flying colors. I failed that part of the test and was not admitted to the prestigious secondary school.

The secondary school to which I was assigned turned out to be a blessing in disguise. In that school, not the worst in the city, there were students from all over the world. I received a multicultural education par excellence. I made many friends, soaked up knowledge like a sponge, and developed into a free thinking, free spirited, and fully alive young woman. The friendships I formed during that time and the experiences that I had nurtured the development of a confident, mature young woman. Living in the memory of that time awakens deep springs of joy in me. I was happy.

It was during that time that I travelled to Europe and became quite proficient in the French language. I camped in Wales for three summers and had many adventures. I was not happy because nothing bad ever happened; I was happy because I was accepted, respected, and loved. I was capable of loving and receiving love without inhibition. My values were clearly defined, and I was not afraid to declare myself for who I was. I was happy.

About three months before my nineteenth birthday, my parents informed me that we were moving back to Jamaica. I was distraught. I was legally an adult, and free to make the decision to stay if I chose to, but my cultural and spiritual values led me to a decision that I have not regretted. I agreed to return to Jamaica but with a plan for returning to England.

When I migrated to England from Jamaica, we travelled by air (a British Airways flight with all the pomp and circumstances that surrounded foreign travel during that time in Jamaica). I was excited about my little blue skirt suit with white collar, white gloves, and my first pair of shoes with half-inch heels. The return to Jamaica was less auspicious. Since we were travelling with a large amount of household goods and furnishings, my mother and I travelled by ship. My father would follow months later by air.

The huge liner was the perfect setting for my lively imagination. I was an avid reader and soon transferred all the mystery and excitement of the books that I had read to the scenes and experiences of the journey across the Atlantic Ocean on this ship. My intense sadness at saying goodbye to England and my childhood friends was soon alleviated by my buoyant young spirit of adventure, the exhilaration of the Atlantic journey, and safe arrival into balmy Caribbean waters. The storm at sea was a novel and exhilarating experience for me, and the mixed emotions of travelling that historic route overshadowed any feelings of sorrow that I might have had.

I was amazed at the intense visceral response to seeing my country again. That year, 1973, was an exciting time in Jamaican political and social development. The rhythm of my heart matched pace with the rhythm of my lovely island home. Old familiar smells assailed my senses and took priority over my memory of the delicate autumn scents that lingered with me from the Southampton dock, where I said goodbye to England and goodbye to a British way of life. I was home.

Despite the joy and fulfillment that came with being home, I was assailed with a sense of fear and unfamiliarity as we travelled by road through the night into the countryside. Seeing roadside food stands and men returning from their fields with machetes in their hands reminded me of pictures I had seen of African villages. I was awed and excited, yet frightened. I was a Jamaican woman with a British heart.

It did not take long for me to revert to the Jamaican way of life. I loved it. I appreciated it more than my friends who had lived all their lives in Jamaica. I wanted everything Jamaican. I could not get enough of the food, the sunshine, the flowers, the customs, and the people. I reveled in my "Jamaicanness" and vowed never to leave it again. The appeals of my friends for me to return to England became less convincing, less alluring, and less desirable. The time came when I knew that I would never return to England.

I spent a year in the youth service program teaching in a rural elementary school. Words almost fail me to describe how happy and full of life I was. I understood myself and loved my life. I did extremely well with my teaching assignment. I was born to teach. My subsequent college experience in Mandeville was instrumental in shaping the adult woman that I would become.

It was in Jamaica that I met the true love of my life. By then, I was mature enough to understand the dynamics of a mature relationship mind and make meaningful decisions. I loved him with passion and intensity tempered by reasoned decision-making. This man who would later become my husband was strong, sensitive, idealistic, deeply spiritual, traditional yet unconventional, and oozing with sex appeal. All other possibilities faded into the background as I started this lifetime adventure, and I have never looked back.

Our wedding was a relatively simple but memorable affair. I wanted a traditional Jamaican wedding with the reception held outdoors at my parents' home. I did not want a rented hall or any of the contemporary trappings. This was to be a spiritual union, void of anything crude or superficial. So, we were married among our dearest friends and members of our family. This was another high point of my life that was distinguished by exquisite, unblemished happiness.

Five months later, our happiness was suddenly marred by the unexpected death of my beloved father. For the first time that I could remember, my prayer was not answered in the affirmative. I have never known such anguish. My life was shrouded in darkness and saturated with uncompromising pain. The tender love of my husband, that wonderful, gentle man, nourished me back to life. Amazingly, I recovered my equilibrium and continued to live.

Young love and optimism brought joy back to my life, and I turned my face to the sky again. God rained down multiple blessings into our lives. We were blessed with love, friends, dreams, and ambitions. We worked hard, struggled a lot, and loved intensely. It was a time of God's smiles.

When children came into our lives, our happiness was intensified. We did not take parenting for granted, mostly because, for a long time, we thought that we would not become parents. The memories associated with my children's childhood days evoke tender smiles and pleasant laughter. We had a good time. Our family unit was tightly knit. I have been surrounded all my life with love, and it has sustained me through difficult times. It has also insulated me from some of the more debilitating psychological effects of migration.

Having a strong biological family as well as very deep ties to a church family has sheltered me during many storms. The psychological effects of migration have had limited effects on me because of these powerful ties. Whether living in Jamaica, England, or the United States of America, my social support has always resided in a Jamaican family and a predominantly West Indian church congregation. My family has always favored life in the suburbs, but we have remained in faithful attendance at a church located in the city of Philadelphia. There are many other churches of the same denomination that are in closer proximity to our home, but we continue our attendance because of the large number of West Indians that attend that church. Many of the events of American society seem far away and barely real because of this deep insulation provided by my social network of family and church friends. The negative aspect of that might be that, if my church friends fail me, I have very few resources outside on which to call for emotional or other help. I have been somewhat successful in widening my social circle to include both Black Americans and Caucasian Americans.

This affiliation with American influences has been achieved in my life mostly through professional contacts. The number of African American friends is greater than the number of Caucasian friends, but still not as many as West Indian friends. This is not due to racism or ethnocentrism on my part; it just feels natural. It is easier to speak in my own voice when with West Indian friends than to constantly adjust my speech and my way of being with my American friends. Lately, I have found myself speaking in my own voice with American friends, not attempting to adjust, but expecting to be accepted "as is."

The way I live my life and the values that I hold dear are fundamentally Jamaican. I am an American citizen with a Jamaican mentality. It is difficult for me to assume the role of "American." I feel like an outsider, so I tend to behave like an outsider. For example, I have never tried to assume an American accent. It has often been a point of wonder to people I meet when they learn that I have lived more years outside of Jamaica than in Jamaica, yet I still maintain a distinct Jamaican accent. As a child and teenager living in England, I spoke with an upper-class British accent. Not very long after returning to Jamaica, I discarded that accent and assumed a Jamaican accent. It was at this time of my Jamaican rebirth that I consciously resumed the use of my native accent and purposed never to lose it again. Nowadays, I laugh at myself when I unintentionally take on an African American way of speaking or a British intonation in response to my immediate surroundings or the company that I am in. It is even more amusing when some people try to determine my place of origin and become confused by the multiple inflections that often emerge in my speech. Like a woman who has lost her virginity, I can never again be purely Jamaican.

Within myself, I feel completely Jamaican. Interestingly, some Jamaicans perceive me as not completely Jamaican, nor completely British, nor completely American. This hodge-podge cultural fabric of my being has resulted in fear of not being accepted as Jamaican enough, British enough, or American enough. It seems that the longer I remain in a foreign country, the more difficult it is for me to embrace a distinct cultural pattern of behavior. I am a conglomerate of all three cultures to which I have been exposed for significant periods of time. Though I wish to deny it, the fact is that I will never regain that cultural part of me that is missing because of my missed years of Jamaican cultural development that is not replicable at a later age. The voices that inform my decisions carry various inflections and intonations, so my behavior tends to bear the imprint of all three cultures.

As I get older, I find it tedious to accommodate these various styles. I balk at having to constantly walk the walk of another, talk another woman's talk, and even think another woman's thoughts. I want to sing my own song, walk my own walk, and talk my own talk. I am a loyal American citizen with a British-West Indian worldview and a heart that is Jamaican. I know that I will never again be purely Jamaican, and I mourn that loss.

On my return to live in Jamaica at age nineteen, I was surprised to discover my status as that of "native foreigner." I would not admit it to anyone, but I was haunted by fear. I had no idea how to be a Jamaican woman. My heart was Jamaican, but my behavior was British. I was a Black Jamaican with a British mind. I was relatively safe within the protected context of the college environment. The college was a multicultural community in which I could safely practice being me. Upon graduation, I was thrust into the role of adult Jamaican woman, but I did not know what that meant. I had spent my entire adolescence and part of my childhood living in London. My predominantly West Indian church community provided the setting for me to maintain my Jamaican identity, but my school, home community, peer group, reading material, and the media taught me a British way of thinking and behaving. It was something of a relief to migrate again about a year after graduating from college. Even though it was a completely new cultural environment, at least I could be Jamaican without the pressure of being a completely authentic Jamaican. "They" would not know the difference. I did not realize that I was trading one identity crisis for another!

A consequence of my migration experiences is an enduring ambiguity between who I perceive myself to be and how others perceive me. Jamaicans tend to regard me as not quite Jamaican. I feel that I have had three distinct life histories— Jamaican, British, and American. My speech reflects that dilemma. To the Jamaican, I sound completely Jamaican, so I am expected to behave in a completely Jamaican way. When I fail to do so, some people become confused or resentful. To the American, I sometimes sound British, and I am comfortable with this characterization while I am with them, but in my heart, I am Jamaican and want to be Jamaican. Sometimes, I just don't quite know how to do the Jamaican me outside of my mind. I have spent the largest segment of my life (forty+ years) in the United States and boast citizenship in this complex society, but I have never internalized an American identity. This is perhaps explainable by the fact that I migrated to the United States as an adult. I am occasionally startled to observe myself speaking and behaving in an "American" way. I am always comforted back to reality when someone tells me that I sound Jamaican. I am Jamaican. I am British. I am American.

I am American, but what does that mean? I am a citizen, but am I African American or Jamaican-American? Here we go again! The ubiquitous question— who am I? Just as before, I enjoy the continuity of a Jamaican identity through affiliation with a predominantly West Indian church community. As usual, I'm not Jamaican enough to be totally acceptable. I dare not intentionally display my British self in that environment because it is meaningless there and unacceptable. When I inadvertently let slip that part of me, I receive immediate and intense retribution from my Jamaican "friends." I then quickly retreat with humble apology and try to be more Jamaican. Outside of that protected environment, I am African American. I truly have little concept of how to negotiate that persona. I can navigate the accent in jest but would feel fraudulent to use it in everyday encounters with others, yet it is expected of me. That and other expectations of African American ethnic identity are beyond my capabilities for being flexible.

So, to the African American, I am once again a native foreigner. I look the part, but I can't talk the talk or walk the walk.

So, I walk gingerly through the cultural morass of my ethnic experiences, trying to adjust to my setting and satisfy the expectations of my immediate environment. Still, I am never quite enough of any of these identities to completely fit in. I understand and like myself as I am, but I seem unexplainable to the world. I am a native foreigner everywhere I go. If I were less introspective, then this dilemma would be easier to solve. Indeed, it might not even be a dilemma. However, I am that person, and I can only do me. Which me? I must be all that I am because all that I am is who I am.

Chapter Three

Jamaican Culture and Migration History

Jamaican presence and contributions in the United States of America have been significant. In fact, Jamaican contributions to diverse areas of American society is out of proportion to its relatively diminutive size. A Jamaican might be tempted to say, "Wi likkle but wi talawah" (We're small but mighty).

"To be Jamaican is to be multicultural since Jamaican culture is such an exotic mixture of many cultural associations. The combination of influences emerged from a long history of different forms of migration to Jamaica" (Marshall, 1987).

The Indigenous Arawak and Taino people were the initial inhabitants of Jamaica. Following the 1494 expeditions of Christopher Columbus, the island became a Spanish colony. The natives of the island died in large numbers from diseases, and as a result, the Spanish brought African slaves over to provide labor. The island remained as a colony of Spain until 1655 when the British took over the Island and gave the name Jamaica. As a British colony, Jamaica became one of the leading exporters of sugar, and it was heavily reliant on African slave labor. In 1838, slavery was banned in the British Empire, and the freed blacks chose to engage in subsistence farms in Jamaica as opposed to working in the plantations. From the early 1840s, the British used the Indian and Chinese indentured labor to work on sugar cane plantations. In 1962 Jamaica obtained its independence from the British. (Sawe, 2019)

Jamaica is comprised of people of African, Indian, Chinese, European, and Middle Eastern descent. There has been a great deal of intermarriage that resulted in Jamaicans of mixed heritage. Jamaica's national motto, *"Out of Many One People,"* reflects the national intention to co-exist with mutual regard and respect. If you have met one Jamaican, you don't necessarily have a full knowledge of what it means to be Jamaican. Individual life experiences, socio-economic standing, level of education, and migration experiences are some of the factors that contribute to the cultural texture of the life of any Jamaican.

There is a sense of solidarity and continuity among Jamaicans across the diaspora. The experience of being a native Jamaican penetrates deeply into the developing mind of a child so that the early childhood values and understanding of life are indelibly imprinted and powerfully resistant to reshaping by means of acculturation. Jamaicans seem to live with the understanding that, once a Jamaican, you are always a Jamaican.

A key indicator of the *once a Jamaican always a Jamaican* attitude of Jamaican immigrants is reflected in the use of language. There is an almost indefinable pleasure associated with resorting to the use of Jamaican patois in private or public dialogue. It is a way of connecting deeply with another Jamaican. It declares our unique identity and captures levels of communication that are inaccessible to the non-Jamaican listener.

"Language is one of the most important parts of any culture. It is the way by which people communicate with one another, build relationships, and create a sense of community."

(Holmes, Greenheart International, 2021)

Language is deeply embedded and revered as a part of Jamaican identity. Jamaicans connect meaningfully with each other using our native patois. This native patois is a blend of African, Arawak, Spanish, and English words. The degree to which Jamaicans maintain their use of the native patois is sometimes an indication of their level of acculturation. Jamaicans tend to assume the speech patterns of those with whom they converse in formal verbal discourse but revert to the native patois when speaking with other Jamaicans. This code switching is sometimes a source of humor among Jamaicans (Lalla, et al., 1990). In former years, the use of patois was frowned upon by middle- and upper-class Jamaicans who tended to favor British speech and mannerisms while denouncing native behaviors, beliefs, or lifestyle of Black Jamaicans. Since the awakening of nationalism that took place in the 1970s, Jamaican patois, cuisine, and music are held in high esteem among all classes of Jamaicans.

Migration and multicultural exposure are integral concepts of Jamaican life. This trend of heavy migration from Jamaica has occurred for varying economic, political, and ideological reasons across the years. Fluctuations in this trend have been influenced significantly by policies and attitudes of host countries. The Migration Policy Institute reports indicate a decline in Jamaican migration to the United States since 2000. This decline is partly due to changing immigration policies. *"The Caribbean is the most common region of birth for the 4.5 million Black immigrants in the United States, accounting for 46 percent* of the total. Jamaica (16 percent) and Haiti (15 percent) are the two largest origin countries for Black immigrants."

"The documented history of Black emigration from Jamaica and other Caribbean islands into the United States dates back to 1619 when twenty voluntary indentured workers arrived in Jamestown, Virginia, on a Dutch frigate. They lived and worked as "free persons" even when a Portuguese vessel arrived with the first shipload of blacks enslaved in 1629" (Murrell, 2024).

> When the first group of immigrants, the Spaniards, arrived in Jamaica, they found the Indigenous Arawak Indians. These native Jamaicans were completely wiped out by the Spaniards through slavery and unfamiliar illnesses. Over the years, between the Spanish invasion and the abolition of slavery, the country became inhabited by numerous immigrant groups including Spaniards, Portuguese Jews, Welsh, Irish, Scottish, English, Germans, and West Africans. Migration of West Africans to Jamaica was unique in that it was forced migration produced by slavery. The Spaniards were the first to bring West African slaves to Jamaica. In 1655 the British invasion shifted power from the Spaniards and the British slave trade supplied more West African inhabitants on the island. British rule continued for 300 years, and today the British culture remains the dominant influence in Jamaican society. (Levine, 1987; Stewart, 1992, Segal, 1995, Lalla , et al., 1990, Segal, 1987, Meeks, 2004).

"After slavery was abolished in Jamaica in 1834 other ethnic groups such as Indian and Chinese arrived on the island as indentured *workers to take the place of African slave labor"* (Lalla & D'Costa, 1990; Segal, 1987).

In 1962, Jamaica became an independent nation. Contemporary Jamaica reflects its diverse history in a population that is comprised of Black Jamaicans of African origin, Indians, Europeans, Chinese, and Middle Easterners. In contemporary Jamaica, the British influence is still present but much less noticeable, and more recently, there is a growing American influence.

> *Jamaicans are currently the largest group of immigrants from the English-speaking Caribbean living in the United States. The migration of Jamaicans to other countries has historically been prompted by economic and educational goals. Like other immigrants to the United States, Jamaican immigrants are usually seeking a better life. During World War II, some Jamaicans migrated to the United States in response to American recruitment of Jamaicans to alleviate labor shortages brought on by the war. . . . After Jamaica gained independence from British rule in 1962, the immigration laws changed so that fewer people were migrating to England. Increased numbers of Jamaicans chose to migrate to the United States instead. (U.S. Library of Congress, 2003).*

Migration is an integral part of Jamaican life, but it has been both a blessing and a hardship.

> *The "brain drain" forms a chronic feature of the Jamaican economy—a permanent sapping process of much needed*

> labor—not simply an occasional event capable of being explained primarily by the political position of a particular politician. The increases in the migration rates of professional, technical, administrative, and managerial workers, and skilled craftsmen in 1977 and 1978 did not herald a new event; high rates of migration for these categories of workers have existed for several years. The volume and the composition of the actual Jamaican migrant population are decided in the main by legislation in other parts of the world. Although Jamaica's population problem has been eased over the years by as much as fifty percent of the country's natural increase being removed by migration, many of those who left were of the type whose skills might have contributed to the national economy—and in ways that might have created employment for others. The economic pull of loss of skilled labor is a permanent feature (Cooper, 1985).

Jamaican migration to the United States has been mostly voluntary, but to some degree, it has also been involuntary. For example, migration since the 1970s has been prompted largely by fear of political instability, diminished healthcare resources, and violent crime. Fear is a powerful force that keeps Jamaicans living in America often contrary to their deepest desires. When individuals are "forced" to adapt to living conditions that they do not necessarily desire, the experience is qualitatively different from that of persons who migrate willingly. The resulting stress can have an adverse effect on the well-being of such individuals.

In the 1970s and early 1980s Jamaica became *"embroiled internally with political unrest and an increase in crime. The political unrest affected all segments of society and destabilized the country significantly. There was an air of fear and mistrust. Hordes of people migrated to other countries to escape the violence and instability. There was a mass exodus of mostly well-educated middle-class Jamaicans"* (US Library of Congress, 2004).

"Some Jamaicans were so alarmed by the sociopolitical climate at the time that they "left their personal effects and settled for a lower standard of living, and the challenge of career change in the United States" (Kessler, et al., 1982).

Vestiges of the political unrest and destabilization of the country during the 1970s and early 1980s can be seen in the "violence, drug trafficking, and economic disarray that continues to motivate Jamaicans to migrate to the United States" (Segal, 1995).

Interviews with Jamaicans living in the United States elicit feelings of nostalgia, loss, and frustration, but Jamaicans continue to migrate in great numbers. Given the level of homesickness and ethnocentrism expressed by Jamaican immigrants, it is surprising that Jamaican migration continues to increase.

The number of Jamaican immigrants to the United States has continued to rise dramatically each year. *"In spite of the high price of adjustment, including cultural and emotional alienation, racial discrimination, mental and physical stress, dead end jobs, and poverty cycles Jamaicans continue to leave their country in search of a better life"* (Segal, 1987).

Given the level of nostalgia, regret, and vestiges of grieving that is heard in discourse with Jamaicans, it seems evident that migration for them is only partially voluntary. The longing for home and the incomplete acculturation is also evident in the practice of many Jamaican families taking the bodies of their deceased relatives back to Jamaica for burial.

When faced with racial prejudice and other hardships that accompany immigrant status in the United States, Jamaicans resort to their sense of belonging and ownership in their native country to help them maintain a sense of well-being.

Jamaicans are proud people. The concept of minority status is foreign to their way of thinking. *"Jamaican migration experience appears to be a mixed blessing. Encounter with racial prejudice is a particularly difficult pill for Jamaican immigrants to swallow"* (Kessler, et al., 1982). According to the small number of researchers who have examined the experience of Jamaican migration to the United States, the racial prejudice and negative connotations associated with African American identity has been a dominant reason for Jamaicans' resistance to assimilation. (Waters, 1994; Kessner, et al., 1982).

A question frequently posed to Jamaicans is, Why did you leave your beautiful country to come to America?

> *Jamaicans migrate to the United States for many socio-economic reasons. Migration is encouraged by economic hardship caused by a failing economy based upon plantation agriculture, lack of economic diversity, and scarcity of professional and skilled jobs. Since the nineteenth century Jamaica has had a very poor land distribution track record. The uneven allotment of arable crown lands and old plantations left farmers without a sufficient plot for subsistence or cash crop farming, which contributed to high unemployment statistics and economic hardship. During the 1970s the standard of living declined due to economic inflation and low salaries. When companies*

and corporations lost confidence in Michael Manley's Democratic Socialist government and his anti-American rhetoric and close business ties to Cuba, the flight of capital from Jamaica and the shift in U.S. capital investments worsened the situation. Jamaica's huge foreign debt and the International Monetary Fund's (IMF) restructuring of the economy further exacerbated the island's economic woes in the 1980s and 1990s. An increase in crime, fueled by unemployment and aggravated by the exporting of criminals from the United States back to Jamaica, forced thousands of Jamaicans to flee the island for safety. Today, unemployment and under-employment continue to rise above 50 percent, wages continue to fall, the dollar weakens, and the cost of goods and services continues to increase. (Murrell, 2023)

The prevailing view of immigrants is that they left their country to seek improved economic conditions in the United States. Although this is one of the reasons for Jamaican migration, only a few realize that dream. For the majority, there is no milk and honey in the promised land. According to one researcher, "*Some Jamaicans have benefited from higher incomes, and access to a greater variety of educational opportunities, but they just as often endure cultural and emotional alienation, racial discrimination, mental and physical strain, dead-end jobs, and poverty.... There is much nostalgia for home amidst recognition that life is better if harder*" (Segal, 1987, p. 59).

The psychological toll on the well-being of Jamaicans living in the United States is significant. Maintaining Jamaican identity is a coping mechanism that aids adjustment while, at the same time, hinders assimilation. Because they cherish the hope of eventual repatriation, McGoldrick (1996) documents that many Jamaican immigrants regard their migrant status as temporary. Furthermore, they can maintain contact with their home culture because of the proximity of Jamaica to the United States (Segal, 1987). It is not clear if this continuity is a positive or negative factor in Jamaican adjustment to American society. Some researchers (Levine, 1987; McGoldrick, 1996) have found that adjustment and acculturation is hindered by not fully relinquishing the original culture. Others would argue that continuity provides resources for coping successfully with acculturation stressors that challenge feelings of psychological well-being (Utsey, et al., 2002; Buddington, 2002). In any case, the restless nature of these weary travelers is evident in their discourse when asked to articulate their migration experiences.

Chapter Four

Jamaican Voices

West Indian American

Alan ran quickly across the yard as the early morning sun warmed his light brown body and the fragrance of hibiscus and bougainvillea perfumed the air around him. Soon, he heard his mother calling for him to come inside for breakfast. The sweet aroma of callaloo, green bananas, and mint tea made his mouth water in anticipation. After helping with his chores around the house, he settled down at the kitchen table to do his homework. His parents were very serious about him doing his homework and generally doing well in school. They believed that, for their children to rise above their humble circumstances, it was important for them to go to school and get a good education. After doing his homework, Alan would go outside again to play. Life was fun and exciting. Alan enjoyed making up games, playing with the other children, and creating toys out of everyday objects that he could find. Alan's life was that of a typical ten-year-old Jamaican boy whose parents belonged to the working class during the 1950s and 1960s.

Alan recalls a happy childhood in a structured home environment with relatively few but immutable rules. He was about seven or eight the first time that he broke the curfew. He was not allowed to enter the house. He was locked out! Alan climbed gingerly into a truck that was parked outside on the side of the road. It was a steel body truck. That night, he slept on two sheets of newspaper in that big, empty truck. He recalls how cold it was, but the lesson that he learned from that was never, ever again to miss curfew. He knew the clear boundaries and expectations of his parents.

As a teenager living in Jamaica, he and his friends were interested in how they were going to change the world. They talked about geopolitical ideologies and how they were going to play a role in trying to change the world. They spent time wrestling with questions of morality and the issues of the day. Alan's migration to the United States at age eighteen was quite an adjustment for Alan. He was ahead of his class academically, but he was far behind his peers socially and completely unready for the cultural adjustment. He wondered at the privilege and what he describes as materialism of his peers. He felt lonely and "different" because of his clothes, his accent, and his lack of knowledge about teenage norms in the United States. He was teased and bullied.

Another area of adjustment for Alan was the weather. He was accustomed to the warm tropical climate of Jamaica and found the stinging cold of a December afternoon in 1974 more than challenging. On his first full day in Philadelphia, Alan kept adding layers of clothing as he tried to explore the neighborhood, but he just could not get warm enough to feel comfortable. Over the next few months, he suffered from the cold while taking public transportation to and from school. Alan longed for home and wondered if his parents had made the right decision in moving the family to the United States. He was homesick.

Alan had his first encounter with racism when he became friends with a Caucasian girl at school. He was allowed to talk to her at school but was not allowed to visit her home. Alan did not understand the whole idea of different races and limits based on the color of one's skin. He could not understand why he wasn't able to go to any barber to get a haircut. The whole racial issue was very confusing for this adolescent boy from Jamaica.

Now, several years later, he has successfully navigated the process of acculturation. When asked to define himself culturally, Alan said that he is West-Indian American. This indicates a blending of cultural norms to accommodate the culture of origin and the host culture. In observing Alan over time, this blending of cultures was evident in many aspects of his daily life. In Berry's model of acculturation, the result of this adaptation strategy produces biculturalism. Alan revealed that he had consciously attempted to identify as African American but found so many barriers to acceptance that he decided to maintain his West Indian identity while also embracing mainstream American culture. Alan said, "I feel strongly that I need to identify myself as a West Indian American as opposed to an African American, not that I disdain African Americans in any way, I know I just feel I'm a West Indian American."

Assimilation

Magda is a petite and elegant woman in her late sixties. She lives in a suburban
neighborhood bordering the city of Philadelphia in Pennsylvania. She speaks with what sounds at first like a British

accent, although she has never lived in the United Kingdom. As I conversed with her further, her accent became distinctly Jamaican. When we talked about her memories of Jamaican food, she unexpectedly began to speak Jamaican patois and tears filled her eyes.

Magda left Jamaica when she was twenty years old. She joined her family in the United States in response to her mother's wishes. She had completed two years of college in Jamaica and intended to complete her studies in Pennsylvania. She intended to become a nurse and then return to Jamaica to work as a nurse. She achieved her goal of becoming a nurse, but she regrets that it took her longer than necessary because she did not understand the educational system and how to navigate that system. Since she had no one to explain how to get things done, she wasted a lot of time pursuing interim goals that were not necessary.

Magda found the transition to life in the United States of America very difficult. She was disappointed. America was not as she expected it to be. She describes her first response to being in America as a state of shock. She disliked the buildings which "looked like prisons" to her.

> "I was used to wide open spaces. I was used to being outside. We had a big yard at home and here the houses were joined together. When I came it was July, so it was hot, but there was nowhere to go. No beach, no yard. I hated it." Magda

The immigration system often necessitates serial migration in which a parent migrates first, leaving the other parent and the children behind. After varying periods of time and a plethora of paperwork, the spouse and children follow. That was the case for Magda's family. Magda was happy to see her mother who she had not seen for seven years, but she missed her friends. She was startled by the appearance of the place that looked so different from pictures that she had seen. There was nothing that excited her about being in America. Her disappointment was palpable. She was lonely and utterly miserable.

It was affiliation with a church community that finally made the adjustment bearable for Magda. She joined a church where she felt very welcome. She met persons in her age group, and she was mothered by older women. She had found a church family, a place where she felt that she belonged. Magda resigned herself to "do her time, finish her education, and return home as soon as possible".

Magda continued to struggle for a long time with the food, the language, and her first exposure to racial prejudice. Except for the brief respite that church attendance offered, she could not find any redeeming qualities in the place that she was expected to now call home.

One year after her arrival in Philadelphia, Magda met the man who would become her husband. That pivotal encounter marked the turning point for Magda in the acculturation process. Together with her husband, a West Indian but not Jamaican, Magda adjusted to life in America and has assimilated so completely that she no longer regards herself as a Jamaican. "I am an American. I am not Jamaican. I have no ties back in Jamaica. My family are all here, or in England or Canada. I'm an American. I'll never go back to Jamaica to live. I wouldn't fit in. I wouldn't know what to do. I've lost touch with Jamaica and what's going on there."

Magda no longer cooks Jamaican dishes, but she admits that she likes to go to places where Jamaican food is served. She has adopted American cultural norms in all areas of her life.

Assimilation is an interesting phenomenon for Jamaicans. Although Jamaicans come in all racial groups, most Jamaicans are Black. Prejudice and discrimination directed towards Black people tend to not differentiate between geographical origin. Consequently, a Black Jamaican might choose to identify as American, but the dilemma becomes whether to identify with Black America or White America. Many Jamaicans, while not choosing to sustain their Jamaican identity, tend to resist identifying as African Americans because of the negative connotations associated with being a racial minority in America. Magda's friends are a mix of mostly African Americans and West Indians, and she identifies with Black America.

Magda identified three main reasons for rejection of her Jamaican heritage.

1. She has lost touch with day-to-day life in Jamaica, and her family have all migrated.
2. The rate of violent crime in Jamaica has remained consistently high, and returning residents are targets of crime.
3. The healthcare system is less than optimum.

"I'm not going back to Jamaica to help anyone. Let them help themselves. The same people you go back to try and help they will kill you. People move back there, and people kill them for what they think they have. No, I'm not going back." Magda

Integration and cognitive dissonance

Pauline migrated to Jamaica at age thirteen. Her family experienced serial migration with the mother migrating first, followed by the father, and then the children. Pauline anticipated living in America with a great deal of excitement. In addition to being reunited with her parents, she looked forward to being in a place that she imagined to be a kind of paradise. She was disappointed. Miami was not as she expected it to be.

"I remember driving through the neighborhood and saying to my mom, "Is this it?" I didn't mean to hurt her feelings, but my perception was totally changed. I was disappointed."

Pauline missed being outside. She missed her friends. She remembers the adjustment as "very hard." She cried a lot and was frequently frustrated and upset. Pauline missed her friends and had a lot of difficulty with adjusting to the school system. Pauline found it difficult to make friends. She felt lost and helpless. She recalls walking out of school one day and going home because she was so frustrated with the language, the unfamiliar school, the food, and everything about her new environment. She was miserable. The transition became easier when Pauline made friends with another girl from Jamaica. This friendship helped to improve her experience at school.

At the time of this interview, Pauline had lived in the United States for twenty-nine years. She was ambiguous about her cultural identity. She had grown up in the United States, but she felt a strong affiliation to her original culture. She had some difficulty articulating her feelings about her cultural identity.

She struggled to describe her mixed feelings. *"At heart I'm Jamaican. But socially and in most respects I'm American. Jamaican at heart, but socially I'm American because this is what I know. When I go back home to Jamaica it's an adjustment."* Pauline

She calls herself Jamaican but feels guilty for doing so because she has really lost touch with day-to-day life in Jamaica. She wants to be Jamaican but has gotten used to living in America. When she visits Jamaica, she feels that she must adjust her behavior and her speech, but she has forgotten how to be fully Jamaican. She regards Pennsylvania as her home now, but she wants to be Jamaican. She is uncomfortable with thinking of herself as American.

Pauline's church is a predominantly West Indian community. This has helped to maintain her emotional ties to Jamaican culture, and her children, though born in the United States, have been strongly influenced by their association with the Jamaican community living in Philadelphia. Her children were both raised in this West Indian environment while living and attending school in Philadelphia. *"If you're of Jamaican parents, you're mixed; you're Jamerican. I guess it's because of the way we raised them in our Jamaican background. They really identify as Jamaican."* – Pauline

The ambiguity and confusion about her cultural identity is evident in her responses and reported behavior. In filling out the ever-present racial questions on various forms, she sometimes checks 'other," sometimes 'African American.' Pauline is aware of changing her accent to accommodate being with different groups of people, although she doesn't do it deliberately. She says that people often have difficulty identifying her accent. Pauline is married to a Jamaican who she thinks is much more Jamaican than she is. She is very hesitant to claim herself Jamaican, although she clings to it tenaciously despite her doubts.

I am proud to be a Jamaican. I am proud to be identified as a Jamaican. I kind of consider myself different in some ways because of the way I was brought up. I've been here since I was thirteen. Unfortunately, I was not around Jamaicans growing up. Where I went to school was White and Indians, and a lot of people from the Virgin Islands and England. So, we didn't have any Jamaican that was so Jamaican that we could really identify and keep it going. I never kept up with what was going on in Jamaica. I never did because that was just my life. When I went away to college I was in a mixed culture, not a lot of Jamaicans. A lot of my friends in college were from other islands. My roommate was Jamaican, and the young man I dated was Jamaican, but like me, they came here when they were eight and twelve. So, we were all Americans growing up. I never met a lot of Jamaicans until I came to Philadelphia and started having Jamaican friends.–Pauline

Pauline admits to an internal identity struggle with her ethnic identity.

I don't seem to fit in with either group. When I talk with other Jamaicans, even like my husband, I find that the way they think is influenced by political happenings in Jamaica that I'm totally ignorant of. Everything is political, and you would have had to experience it to understand it. Well, I didn't experience it, so I feel lost when I hear them talking. Politics seems to have influenced the way they think. I don't always feel as if I connect with Jamaicans in that way. I'm always a little uncomfortable with it.–Pauline

The experience of being the child of Jamaican parents while living in the American society at once instills a strong sense of heritage while somehow alienating some Jamaican immigrants from "mainstream" American culture.

My parents' influence as I grew up was Jamaican of course, so I know myself as Jamaican. For example, when we just came here breakfast was a big thing for us. Then I found out that Americans sometimes didn't have breakfast or had junk food for breakfast. We weren't allowed to do that. I remember my mother saying, "You might be living in America, but I will bring you up as a Jamaican." It's funny but I've found myself saying the same thing to my children–Pauline

Over time, the longing to return to Jamaica changes for some Jamaicans. Coerced by circumstances into adapting and acculturating, the Jamaican immigrant eventually loses the hope of returning and adjusts to the realization that they will never again be fully Jamaican. We become native foreigners: Not fully Jamaican anymore but always foreigners in this strange land, we become hybrids of our true Jamaican selves; we are native foreigners while visiting Jamaica, and marginalized foreigners while living in the United States. We are resilient and privileged outcasts with no easy way back home and denied the privilege of full acceptance in our new country.

"*I wanted to go back so badly. I thought that as soon as I was old enough, I would go back. For the first six months that was my dream. After that I started to adapt. Now I'm thinking that Jamaica is not for me. When I'm there I feel lost. I don't know what to do. I'm ready to come back after a week and a half. But I'm Jamaican at heart."–Pauline*

Integration and resilience

Hope is a concept that has the power to motivate and sustain resilience in the face of disappointment and thwarted dreams. Danny left Jamaica with high hopes of achieving financial and academic goals that were difficult for him to realize within the socioeconomic realities of Jamaican life back in the early 1980s. Migration was an exciting experience for this Jamaican man who migrated to the United States as a young adult in his early twenties. The novelty and excitement of a dream fulfilled kept Danny buoyant for the first few years. Hope provided the fuel for his motivation. Resilience provided sustaining power when challenges threatened to shatter his optimistic expectations. Reflecting on the often-painful climb to his currently contented and successful middle-aged life, Danny questions whether he made a successful adjustment to the realities of migration to the United States.

I'm not sure if I made the adjustment. I'm not sure if my adjustment was effective. I think that might be part of why I dropped out of college. If I could have just chosen to be a student and to ignore the family part, then I think I would have survived college. But I don't think I made that adjustment effectively. The main reason for leaving college was that being in college wouldn't allow me to maintain the family aspect of it. I therefore decided to change where we lived. Trying to maintain a home, going to college at the same time; having a job that can maintain a home didn't allow that. Really, it was a failure in adjustment. I think there was a failure in adjustment.–Danny

Despite the challenges of adjustment, Danny does not regret migrating to the United States. He recognizes that life would have been different, and possibly better, if he had not migrated, but he does not negate the tremendous life experiences that might not have occurred if he had remained in Jamaica. Danny's resilient and innovative spirit propelled him to take the hand dealt to him by his socio-economic limitations, coupled with acculturation stress and the realities of living in a racist society, and rise above it all to fulfill his dreams and aspirations. The route he took was different from the one he had imagined and anticipated, but today he has no regrets. He lives in the mature understanding that he is indeed the master of his destiny. The question of ethnic identity creates no confusion for Danny. He is a Jamaican.

I am definitely a Jamaican living in the United States. I still think as a foreigner, a Jamaican foreigner. My accent still betrays me, not reluctantly. My dreams and my hopes and my passion are for my country-- Jamaica. Even though I still find ways to assist and to be helpful and supportive in the culture that I live in the United States, I have great passion for helping and assisting what goes wrong and right in Jamaica. My values are still the values I gained in Jamaica, and sometimes there is a resistance against some of the values I have here compared with those I gained in Jamaica. I'm still a Jamaican."–Danny

For Danny, family values and the role of the father in the family are fundamental principles that have not been altered by acculturation. One of his few regrets is that the American lifestyle does not easily lend itself to supporting time to be with the family, especially for those who struggle financially.

The husband is supposed to be the provider. That's his overall responsibility. Even if he's not making the most money, that's his responsibility, and he's to take care of that at all costs. He's to be present and be a presence among the children and in the family. In the United States I think that there is a more balanced approach. Well, I'm not sure if it's balanced, but a more laissez-faire approach to the male role. It's not as strong and demanding as I had it in Jamaica. I still endorse the Jamaican way in this. I'm not giving that up for the more relaxed role that I see here in the United States. Family time is essential, but the lifestyle here does not always make it easy to spend enough time with the family. In one sense there's constant frustration because there are things that I may want to do or feel that it's necessary to be done, but you're not able to do it. I feel the constant need to go out with the kids, to go to a sporting event, but the time is never there. So, I keep working in an attempt to get more vacation and get more money. There's a constant sense of frustration, not achieving what you know is necessary; constantly being frustrated with not being able to do it or see it come to fruition. There's a constant struggle with frustration. - Danny

Danny's strong sense of ethnic identity is bolstered by his strong Jamaican social network. He is truly a Jamaican living in America. Since Danny functions well in both his native Jamaican culture and his current American environment, Berry would probably describe his adjustment pattern as integrated (Berry, 1992).

I think I understand the American society. I've learned through various means, some by trial and error, and some by painful mistakes. I've learned, and I'm still learning, how to survive in this country. I think I've made great strides in just learning how to survive. I'm not outside of the loop. I'm not on the fringes of the American society. I have a business. I live in a good neighborhood. My kids are attending good schools. I'm pretty much in the mainstream of American society. I'm adjusting properly, interacting with all different levels of the American society. I'm satisfied with that, but I still try to keep up with what's going on in Jamaica. I still have a need to visit and go back and be a part of the future. I'm constantly seeking ways to find my way back into the mainstream of the Jamaican society. I think I've adjusted pretty well to the American society. I think I have a balanced view, a balanced life being a part of both societies. – Danny

However, Danny seems to embrace an element of separation in his pattern of social affiliation.

"Most of my close associates are also Jamaican or of West Indian background. Most of my friendships are associated with my church, and most of my church family are Jamaican or from West Indian background. Almost all my social interactions are with other Jamaicans. My association with non-Jamaicans is mostly in the work setting, and that doesn't affect my social life." – Danny

Danny says that he is happy. Family, friends, church, and hard work make up the fabric of his life. Whether living in the United States or in Jamaica, Danny has always found these things to be the stabilizing forces that give meaning to his life. He longs for home and all things Jamaican, but his strong, resilient, optimistic personality does not leave much time for regrets or second-guessing.

"One thing that this country does is to allow you to be hopeful. Even though your dreams might not have come true yet, I think this country always allows you to see the possibility of the dream. In balancing the frustrations, and the unrealized dreams of the past with the possibilities of the future there is hope and the realization that opportunities still exist." - Danny

Danny's longing for home is balanced by a realistic outlook. Jamaica is still home for Danny, but he is prepared to survive at home or abroad.

The only thing that will prevent me from returning eventually is if Jamaica gets so bad in terms of crime and economics that it wouldn't make sense for me to go back there. But so long as I can guarantee some degree of safety, and while there is some possibility that I can live and not starve to death, returning home will always be a strong possibility. I am concerned for those who don't see themselves as Jamaicans anymore, or those who would totally alienate themselves from Jamaica and from the things that are going on in Jamaica. I am concerned for those Jamaicans who see Jamaica only in negative terms. I think that all Jamaicans need to have a concern for our country and need to actively seek ways to help the people of Jamaica. –Danny

Beverly P. Gordon

Separation

Ruth migrated to the United States of America when she was eighteen years old. She came on an athletic scholarship to study, run track, and then return to Jamaica. Six years after returning to Jamaica, she once again migrated to the United States, this time for economic reasons in the aftermath of a divorce. She was searching for a way to get her life back together. Even now, she describes herself as still searching.

"Socially, Jamaica is just a nicer place to live. You go to the supermarket, and you see several people that you know. While here, you're socially isolated as far as I am concerned. Nobody sees you. Nobody cares. It's neither here nor there. You can really get lost in this society. You don't have a support system."–Ruth

Ruth not only feels socially isolated, but she is also bored.

"In Jamaica there was always something taking place, some form of entertainment.
Anything that's taking place in the rural areas of Jamaica— yam festival, jerk festival.
I was used to always be coming and going. That was just really the life."

Ruth lives in the United States, but she does not feel connected to America or the American lifestyle.

"I am still definitely very Jamaican. I'm a vegetarian, but I cook vegetarian food along Jamaican lines. I tend to go to the Jamaican stores to see what is happening. I haven't really assimilated into this

society. Not at all. I don't consider myself an American although I have a U.S. passport. It's a passport of convenience as far as I am concerned. I only got that passport because of the hassle that they were giving green card holders to come and go. I had my resident status for twenty-something years before I changed it over."

Ruth has family members living in the United States. Her mother migrated to the United States as part of a work program. After working with a family as a caretaker for one of the members, she achieved permanent residence and sent for her children in a serial migration pattern. Despite having family nearby, she continues to feel disconnected and socially isolated. She attributes this phenomenon to the fact that her "family has not assimilated either." She socializes with her family but not outside of her family. She describes life in America as incredibly stressful.

Despite an overarching concern about the high level of crime and violence in Jamaica, Ruth does not see this as a barrier to her returning home to Jamaica. She views the crime issue as partof the growing pains of a developing nation.

"I am hoping that Jamaica will continue to develop. I am hoping that development will lead to peace. It would be wonderful if Jamaica could discover some natural resource. I would love to see a strengthening of the education system even to take it back to the way it was when we were in school. We got solid British education, and that has changed. It might help our situation. I think that might help get rid of some of the illiteracy that we have. We need to get rid of the high level of illiteracy and violence. A lot of our problems stem from that. A third of our population is illiterate. People are not able to reason things out. They just act

without thinking, and so we have increased violence. I'm hoping that Jamaicans here will turn some of their energies towards Jamaica to do what they can. I'm hoping to eventually be able to send a couple of children to school in Jamaica. I don't want to do anything bigger than that.

Ruth has found big differences between parenting in Jamaica and parenting in the United States of America. She says that "our value systems are different. We are still a conservative society in Jamaica compared to this society."

Marginalization and racial trauma

Denise was a nurse in Jamaica. She migrated in response to a recruitment drive by the American health system, for Registered Nurses to migrate to the United States.

"There were free agents that were working for the American health system to help in getting nurses from the Caribbean, India, and Korea. I came with a certain outlook from what I had seen in the movies and read in books, and that sort of thing. But even though I had an awareness of what the society was like, to actually live it day by day is a little bit different. The way America is portrayed on the television is that all the White communities are pristine and beautiful, and then you have the ghettoes. So, I thought that either you had to live in a pristine neighborhood or the ghetto. It took me a while to realize that I was living in a Polish/Italian/Jewish/Greek neighborhood. The subway also was kind of odd. What was most startling to me was the transformation on the streets when 5:00 PM came. It was quite harrowing. It was like

a festering wound that broke open and poured with people who came in an unrelenting flow." Denise

Adjustment to the new culture was a challenge for Denise. The most significant challenge that was presented was in finding a place to live. For the first time in her life, she was confronted with racial prejudice and blatant discrimination. The most incomprehensible evidence of prejudice came for Denise when patients refused her care because of her skin color. Despite her professional skills and experience, she was treated with disdain by both patients and colleagues. Racial prejudice and discrimination became a real deterrent to progress professionally. Denise became discouraged after several attempts to achieve her career goals and gave up. Although Denise would like to return to Jamaica, she is hesitant to do so without having achieved her career goals. She worries about how her colleagues in Jamaica will view her. Since she migrated to improve her career and professional status, she feels that she will be ridiculed if she returns without those achievements.

Denise feels demoralized by her experience of living in America. In response and defense of her self-esteem, she vigorously maintains her identity as a Jamaican.

"I'll never not be Jamaican. I think I am more Jamaican than most Jamaicans that I've met here. I still think in terms of my upbringing, in terms of what the community invested in me, in community living, in familial living. I will never not be primarily Jamaican. It's just— It's absolutely who I am."

Chapter Five

Finding the Way Home

Migration is a phenomenon that challenges our ability to cope with change. The immigrant's challenge is to find a place within the structure of the new society that allows them to retain a cohesive sense of self and attain a functional meaning to their presence in the new society. Failure to achieve these goals results in depletion of well-being. Migration takes its toll on individual development, family dynamics, social commitment, ethnic identity, and psychological well-being. Individuals experience loss, emotional turmoil, frustration, and impaired sense of identity. Family cohesion is threatened by migration practices that separate families for significant periods of time. It might be assumed that individuals who migrate voluntarily do not experience trauma from the experience. This is not necessarily true. The motivation for migrating might override other deeply held values and commitments that conflict with the necessary changes that occur with migration.

Some individuals are better equipped to deal with change and trauma than other individuals. Whether we accept the notion that individuals come into the world hard-wired to tolerate trauma, or we defer to the notion that environmental forces shape the individual to meet the circumstances of their lives, some individuals tolerate change more efficiently than others. Resilience is that phenomenon that allows an individual to tolerate trauma and remain psychologically intact. What factors contribute to the resilience of immigrants who survive the changes and psychological adjustments that accompany migration? While there might well be other resources that contribute to resilience among this immigrant population, the seven individuals who were interviewed expressed two common themes: spirituality and family.

Traditional Jamaican life supports interdependence between family and religious structures to act as socializing agents that provide fundamental values and beliefs by which individuals order their lives. The Jamaican immigrant is tasked with adjusting to a complex, individualistic society in which family and religion are only options among a wide variety of competing voices. Such unfamiliar and often conflicting patterns, relationships, and worldviews can give rise to internal conflicts and adjustment challenges that threaten the immigrant's self-concept, self-efficacy, and self-worth.

When a family member migrates, this event represents a multi-faceted stressor for that family. The most obvious aspect of the stressor is the loss of a family member. The loss is ambiguous because, although the person is no longer present with the family, that individual remains a part of the family and factors into decisions made by the family. The person is not physically present to give or receive input from the rest of the family. There is uncertainty as to when the family will be reunited since they are at the mercies of capricious immigration laws. Even when the family is reunited, the resulting changes from the separation can leave permanent areas of damage or at least challenges that were not present before.

Native Foreigner

The small batch of interviews included in this book demonstrate the fact that migration produces costly psychological collateral damage even when migration is primarily voluntary and perceived as beneficial and necessary. The significance of the impairment might be proportionate to the period of disorganization that ensues as well as the resources available for reorganization or recovery. When pre-existing and ongoing stressors are factored into the equation, migration can be the trigger for intense psychological fallout for both the individual migrant and the family unit to which that migrant belongs. Stressor overload can then become a major demoralizing crisis.

Within the West Indian immigrant community, there is a strong attitude of ethnocentrism. This is particularly noticeable among Jamaicans. They are proud of their heritage, their freedom, their creativity, and their resilience. In their casual conversations, they tend to revert to their local patois dialect which is used by all strata of the Jamaican society. There is much reminiscing and nostalgia among Jamaican immigrants in their social gatherings.

The depth of patriotism and homesickness that is expressed by Jamaican immigrants are inconsistent with the extreme sacrifices that many Jamaicans make to become residents and citizens of the United States. It is difficult to explain the contradiction that is evident in the behavior of Jamaican immigrants to the United States. On the one hand, they are willing to endure extreme hardship and even embarrassment to achieve their goal of becoming American citizens. Many Jamaicans work two or three jobs to enable themselves and members of their families to enjoy the better things of life. Truly, there are Jamaicans who leave their island home with no thought or desire to return. Still, some leave their country with well-devised plans and intentional design, but still yearn for the familiarity and context of "home." They live divided lives, caught between two irreconcilable cultures that both claim their allegiance. On the other hand, while some acculturate and relegate their origins to a place in memory of the past that has little bearing on the present, others strive passionately to retain their original identity while conforming to the expectations of their host environment. Still, others never relinquish any part of their original identity and live estranged lives within a culture where nobody knows their identity. In any case, Jamaican immigrants endure multiple areas of psychological adjustment related to the experience of migration.

Immigration laws often make it difficult, if not impossible, for some Jamaicans to migrate legally to the United States. Rather than accepting life in their home country, some Jamaicans enter the United States illegally. Some eventually achieve legal status while others remain for years with an illegal status. Some Jamaicans have suffered intense emotional trauma because of receiving news of serious illness of family members in Jamaica, as they were compelled to miss seeing their loved ones or attending the funeral when that loved one died. Such tremendous sacrifice to remain in the United States belies the intense longing and devotion that is expressed by Jamaicans living in the United States. This suggests that migration fulfills a deeper need than the need for belonging and for maintaining a predictable environment.

At some level, Jamaican immigrants are reluctant to return home. One of the contributing factors to this reluctance is revealed in the interviews recorded in the previous chapter. Individuals talked about their fear of crime. Given the equally high rate of crime in the United States, it is difficult to believe that Jamaicans migrate to the United States to find relief from high crime rates. It is plausible, though, that the relative size of the two countries produces an illusion of safety produced by the lower probability of being a direct victim of life-threatening criminal activity. The difference in political structure may also lend to this increased sense of security experienced by Jamaicans living in the United States.

What are the factors that motivate Jamaicans to leave their country? The interviews that are recorded in this book highlight three major reasons for Jamaican migration:

1. Economic hardship
2. Academic ambition
3. Fear

The perception prior to migration is that life in the United States of America will produce a higher socio-economic status. The hope is usually that expanded educational opportunities will enable the Jamaican immigrant to obtain a high-paying job. Those for whom this dream is realized are likely to acculturate with little difficulty, and then there is little or no deep longing for home. Those whose dreams are frustrated become resentful and regard their decision to migrate as a huge mistake. Often, these individuals look back at their lives prior to migration and realize that they would have been better off in terms of social status and economic standing had they remained in their country. They are forced to maintain the aura of success when they return to Jamaica for visits because they fear the ridicule and disdain of those who remained in Jamaica. This cognitive dissonance and perpetual stress takes its toll on the physical health and psychological well being of Jamaican immigrants.

This stress is sometimes manifested in the form of such diseases as hypertension, frequent headaches, weight management problems, anxiety, and depression.

Those who seek educational opportunities as their main purpose for migrating also face debilitating challenges. The high cost of education can render educational goals impossible for the Jamaican immigrant who landed with minimal financial resources. Since financial aid is not immediately available for most, the individual must sometimes forgo educational pursuits while desperately trying to make ends meet and provide the necessities of life. The problem is compounded for those who have families to take care of as well. Many times, the grand educational goals with which the person migrated become extinguished by the everyday brutal struggle for survival.

On the other hand, many who migrated for educational purposes become enamored of the financial and professional opportunities available to them in the United States, and they fail to return to their country to render the service that their acquired education would allow them to. This group also tends to adapt and acculturate with a fair amount of ease. For them, the pros of life in the United States outweigh the cons of missing life in their native land. Still, many of them harbor longings for home and promise themselves to return to Jamaica "soon." They talk of Jamaica and reminisce, saying, "When I was back home…" Meanwhile, student loan payments and other necessities of American life keep them bound to their jobs and a way of life that they only partially appreciate.

The Jamaican culture respects education above wealth. A Jamaican parent will sacrifice much to secure the education of their children. In general, Jamaican parents have high academic expectations for their children. It is a rare Jamaican parent who shows no interest in the education of their children. It is difficult for parents who sacrifice their own comfort to give their children the best in education and lifestyle to understand the young person who rejects this offering in favor of the "thug" life or just a life of mediocre performance and achievement. This phenomenon challenges the cognitive consistency of most Jamaican parents.

The picture of the Jamaican immigrant that emerges is that of a restless wanderer who seeks "the promised land" but finds no milk and honey there. A pervasive theme in the conversation of immigrants from Jamaica is their preoccupation and longing for the life that they had "back home." Even those who declare that they have no intentions of returning to Jamaica eventually betray their unconscious nostalgia for "home."

If I were able to turn back the hands of time I would decide not to migrate. It is true that I would never have had the tremendously enriching experiences that I have had. So much of who I am would not exist and that would be a great loss. Yet I often feel that there is a greater loss that I am not even fully aware of because that reality was never allowed to develop. Upon reflection, persons from Jamaica sacrifice too much for the dubious privilege of life in the United States. People leave their professions, their livelihood, their family, their identity, and their sense of wholeness to take on the challenge of social isolation, fragmented identity, loss of social status, racial bigotry, and uncertain ethnic identity when they migrate to live in the United States.

As the saying goes, "The grass always seems greener on the other side of the fence." Nowhere is this truer than in the case of immigrants. I recall my interview at the American Consulate in Kingston, Jamaica. My parents had filed for me to join them in the United States, and it was my turn for the notorious "interview" that would determine whether I would be awarded my permanent visa. The gentleman who interviewed me sat behind an impressive desk that failed in diminishing his warm, friendly attitude. After the formalities had been seen to the gentleman made a comment to me that seemed to be drawn from him against his will. He said, "America is just another place like any other place; it has trees, streets, and life just like here. There's nothing special about being there". After making that statement, he moved on to the rest of his activities without allowing me the opportunity to respond or without any indication of wanting to pursue the topic further. Many years later I understood the message that he was trying to convey to me. The gentleman was African American.

I can only imagine how it must appear to someone who had known the reality of racial prejudice directly or indirectly as a part of the fabric of daily life to see people giving up their freedom and sense of identity and belonging to voluntarily subject themselves to the perpetual status of "other." Unaware of the psychological pitfalls of migration, we celebrate our license to become foreigners to our native land and assume an air of achievement. Once we discover the unequal trade that we have made to obtain our new status, we are too ashamed, too afraid, or too encumbered to disentangle ourselves.

So many of us made this trade at a time when our country needed us most, and we mourn from a distance the loss of so much that we hold dear. Some long to return home but fear for their safety as they have become "native foreigners" in their own country. Was it worth the price? Did our circumstances warrant the brain drain that we created in our country? Even if we gained invaluable experience and expertise, what profit is it to us and the land of our birth?

Some Jamaican immigrants do gain financially from their travels. Most of us simply exchange one level of poverty for another level of poverty. I can't help thinking that my peers who remained in Jamaica are far wealthier in social and psychological resources than those of us who migrated.

I was teaching a course on culture and society when I had a profound experience of innocuous racism. The students in my class were aware of my Jamaican origin as well as my status as an American citizen with thirty-three years of residence in the United States at that time. The class discussion shifted to the topic of drug use. I was immediately confronted with a question about marijuana in the context of my knowledge about the drug as a Jamaican. I was taken aback but maintained my composure. It soon became evident that these students really believed that, as a Jamaican, I must have used marijuana at some time even though I might not use it now. I did my best to convey the fact that I have never even held the substance in my hands let alone used it. To my chagrin, most of the students refused to believe this. I was disappointed to realize that my perception of myself as a well-respected Christian professional was not necessarily shared by others. In the final analysis, I was simply a Black, weed-smoking Jamaican woman! I felt particularly endeared to the few students who maintained their confidence in me as one who "wouldn't do that." At this point in my life, I really don't feel any particularly deep psychological impact from the experience, but my mind still registers mild surprise and a flicker of anxiety.

We sacrifice family cohesion when we migrate. Even if the family is privileged to migrate together, we create multicultural communities within our homes that create intensified generational conflicts. We removed many baby boomers from the fabric of Jamaican society thereby removing a large socializing faction that would help to shape the next generation.

Black Jamaican immigrants sacrifice their freedom and dignity when they migrate to the United States. Despite limited economic opportunities and political uncertainty that has triggered so much migration from Jamaica, the reward of second-class citizenship and racism that the Jamaican immigrant endures is far less desirable. Black Jamaican immigrants do not have the privilege of ever fully assimilating into mainstream society. This resolution is prohibited by the enduring nature of the color of our skin. In America, race is pertinent to every aspect of daily life. Laws have been enacted that limit the perpetration of discriminatory acts, but laws have never been successful as a deterrent against unlawful thoughts that influence behavior. Black Jamaicans are subsumed in the category of people labeled as African Americans. The daily news and the individual experience of Jamaicans living in America speak loudly of the ongoing, pervasive nature of racial prejudice and discrimination in the society.

I am aware of the benefits of travel and exposure to other cultures. I believe that it is good to travel and experience various cultures. It broadens our vision and expands our worldview. I have been enriched by my multicultural exposure. Despite the achievements and benefits derived from migration, I deeply mourn the loss of continuity and the ethnic deprivation that inevitably accompanies migration. Hindsight is more accurate than foresight, so we would probably not have been convinced if anyone had made a serious attempt to dissuade my family from migrating.

Having migrated as a young child, my second migration was easier to agree to because I had already become a native foreigner. Perhaps if I had not migrated the second time, then I would have reintegrated fully.

If called upon to give advice to fellow Jamaicans, I would say: Travel, but go home soon. If you have not left yet, then don't go. If you have already left, go home if you can, and if you cannot go home, then do your best to integrate.

To survive the ravages of being "other" over long periods of time, a person must have inner resources that ensure their emotional survival and sense of well-being. Strong core beliefs and values support such survival. A strong ethnic identity and national pride combined with realistic self-concept and well-grounded sense of worth are key to adjustment and survival of the Black immigrant living in the United States. In many instances, spiritual commitment, wisdom, and vision have provided vital inner resources that allow Black Jamaican immigrants to not only survive but thrive physically, emotionally, and socially.

Migration is an increasing phenomenon. Whereas I believe that maintaining primary residence in one's own country is most amenable to optimum mental health, it is unlikely that migration will cease. The realities of modern society demand attention to developing and maintaining positive adjustment skills and strategies for Black immigrants to the United States.

The psychological impact of migration appears to be a global problem. Individuals from various ethnic backgrounds and countries of origin feel compelled to seek a better life in another country that they perceive as having more resources with which to fulfill their needs. Individuals leave their homes or are forced from their homes, but always with the expectation that life will be better for them in the new country. Often, their expectations are not satisfied.

When optimistic expectations encounter disappointment, immigrants are faced with the challenges of adjustment and coping. Even when expectations are fulfilled, immigrants must still make adjustments that alter their experience of self and relationship to others that is profoundly different from the experience of living in one's native land.

There is a clear difference between the experience of immigrants who fully embrace the new culture and gladly relinquish their native ethnic identity and that of those who merely endure their new environment while all the time longing for home.

Home is defined as one's place of residence, the place of one's birth, or your base. It is where you return to after going out. What does it feel like to be in a place where you are always out, and never experience a sense of coming back to base? There is no medicine for the homesick soul. Only a return home can heal the malady of overwhelming nostalgia and longing that engulfs the homesick heart.

Perhaps the immigrant experience is a reflection of a universal human problem that remains largely unrecognized. Man's relentless pursuit of a better life implies an intuitive knowledge that life was intended to be different from how we currently experience it. The longing for a place to belong and the restless discontent of those who migrate for various reasons is a futile attempt to satisfy a more deep-rooted longing for God and a place called home.

The daily struggle for happiness, and what Maslow calls *self-actualization*, is evident from the mansions and palaces of the wealthy and famous to the shanty towns and hovels of those who battle the evils of poverty. It seems that no matter where man finds himself, he is never fully satisfied or content. There seems to be a longing for something better.

I propose that the real motivation for man's restless spirit and lust for exploration is a longing for a place called home that exists only in the presence of God. The person who has found that sweet assurance of their place in God's heart finds peace, contentment, satisfaction, and hope no matter where on earth they happen to be. The longing for home is not so much for a physical place despite all the natural beauty and treasured memories.

This is not to deny the genuine feelings of homesickness that assail the immigrant from time to time. It is simply to emphasize the fact that the Christian sojourner experiences a sense of peace and contentment based on their relationship with God rather on the fact of being in any geographic location. The Christian believer experiences the common bond with the rest of humanity based on the fundamental belief in God as the creator and sustainer of all people.

In reaching out to those who experience feelings of alienation and loss due to migration stress, it is important to introduce a universal worldview entrenched in the concept of membership in a multicultural family of God. Earthly cultural values and norms give us a sense of identity and foster feelings of belonging but become problematic when these values and norms conflict with the larger society in which we live.

The culture of Christian love and brotherhood reduces such cultural miscommunications, misunderstandings, and bias. There is no firmer foundation on which to build one's sense of self and perception of self in relation to others than the Christian worldview.

Within the Christian culture, the concept of home takes on a different meaning. Home is a place where we experience complete acceptance, reconciliation, and restoration. The Christian knows that he is home when he experiences peace with God and man. The songwriter was able to say, "Anywhere with Jesus I can safely go" because he understood that home is where we find ourselves in the presence of God.

Home— a warm and comforting word that conjures up happy memories for some and feelings of sadness and despair in others. Home— the place where we learn to love ourselves and others or we learn feelings of worthlessness and mistrust. Home— where hearts are united and individuals feel safe physically and emotionally. Home was intended to be a place of love, comfort, joy, and unencumbered expression of our unique personalities. I remember that when I was a little girl my mother had a lamp with a glass shade that had the words, "Home Sweet Home," written on it. Home is the place that lights the path of little children to their future and nourishes the hearts and lives of all who belong to the circle. Home is where you don't have to wonder if you'll be accepted; you just accept the fact that you are.

Human beings need acceptance and the emotional security of affiliation to a stable social support network. Immigrants, particularly dark-skinned immigrants, struggle to find affirmation, acceptance and belonging— a place that they can call home. Too frequently they meet with misunderstanding, prejudice, mistrust, and hatred. Without a place to call home, individuals lose a sense of cultural identity and psychological well-being. Affiliation with a Christian community can contribute to developing resilience among Jamaican immigrants. Persons who feel disconnected, misunderstood, or different from others will not easily maintain fellowship and are more likely to engage in self-destructive behavior. Jamaicans have a rich social and spiritual heritage that imparts a sense of dignity and purpose to life. Tapping into this heritage can be instrumental in alleviating the stress that accompanies migration and acculturation.

The belief that they are a part of a larger community of believers who envision a better home to come while currently enjoying a sense of home through their spiritual experiences enhances the immigrant's experience and frees them to become meaningful, civic-minded citizens of their new country. For the Christian immigrant, home is the heart of God. They might miss the familiarity of their native country, but they can find rest and fulfillment in the heart of God, which is big enough to encompass the whole earth. If the heart of God is home, then the Christian can be at home anywhere because God is everywhere. In God, Christians find a permanent source of security, acceptance, and belonging. It was Augustine who said, "Thou hast made us for thyself, and our hearts are restless till they find their rest in thee."

Chapter Six

Homecoming

I had the distinct pleasure of visiting Jamaica in June 2019, exactly forty years after first migrating to the United States of America. It had been eight long years since my last visit. This time, I returned for the 8th biannual Diaspora Conference. I am deeply satisfied with the service that we rendered while there. On a personal level, I experienced a significant identity breakthrough that marks a pivotal point in my life experience. For the nine days of my stay in my homeland, I experienced myself completely and irrevocably as one hundred percent Jamaican. I felt thoroughly embraced and known by my people.

I have come to a time in my life when I will not be denied the opportunity to be all that I was designed to be. There is no apology in my heart for living in a place that is not the place of my birth. Every experience has brought me to this time. As never before, I realize that the world might never know my name or recognize my face, but I will not pass through this world without being known and without touching the lives of all with whom I come in contact. I won't look down or look away. I am here by design in whatever place I happen to be. What is the point of being here if I don't do something about something or say something about anything? My place on earth is not determined by national or international law. My place on earth is determined by the will of God to whom I yield every aspect of my being. I've lived what is likely the longest part of my life already. What the future years lack in length will be amply made up for in volume and substance.

Ignorance pervades the mind of man. We are ignorant of the meaning of our existence. Surely there can be no meaning in simply waking up, eating, sleeping, excreting, suffering a lot, enjoying life to varying degrees, then dying. To experience the profound meaning of our existence we must surely live for something outside of and bigger than ourselves. We must immortalize the essence of who we are by sharing all that we are with every person that we are able to reach. We must look honestly into the eyes of men, women, and children of every 'race,' creed, and national origin. Soul must touch soul and heart must reach heart. I love my country for all that it is and the hopes of what it can become, but I am a pilgrim with entry rights to every country and every part of God's wonderful earth. For now, I may sometimes have to suffer being a native foreigner, but I am citizen of the world— a world created by God with a particular place and time reserved just for me.

References

Berry, J.W. (1997), Immigration, Acculturation, and Adaptation. Applied Psychology, 46: 5-34. https://doi.org/10.1111/j.1464-0597.1997.tb01087.x

Buddington, S. A. (2002). Acculturation, psychological adjustment (stress, depression, self-esteem) and the academic achievement of Jamaican immigrant college students. International Social Work, 45 (4) 447-464).

Cooper, D. W. (1985), Migration from Jamaica in the 1970s: political protest or economic pull? International Migration Review. 1985 Winter;19(4):728-45.

Ferguson, G. M., Iturbide, M. I., & Gordon, B.P. (2014), Tridimensional (3D) acculturation:
ethnic identity and psychological functioning of tricultural Jamaican immigrants.
International Perspectives in Psychology: Research, Practice, Consultation 3(4), 238-251.

Holmes, K. (2021), Language: The essence of culture. https:// greenheart.org/blog/greenheart-international/language-the-essence-of-culture/

Kessner, T., & Caroli, B. B. (1981). *Today's immigrants, their stories.* New York: Oxford University Press.

Lalla, B. & Dcosta, J. (1990). Language in exile. Knoxville, Tennessee: University of Alabama Press.

Levine, B. B. (1987). Surplus populations: economic migrants and political refugees. In B. B. Levine (Ed.), *The Caribbean Exodus* (pp. 15-31). New York: Praeger Publishers.

Marshall, D. (1987). A history of West Indian migrations: Overseas opportunities and safety- valve policies. In B. B. Levine (Ed.), The Caribbean Exodus (pp. 15-31). New York: Praeger Publisher

McCoy, T. L. (1987). A primer for U.S. policy on Caribbean migration: Responding to pressures. In B. B. Levine (Ed.), The Caribbean Exodus (pp. 15-31). New York: Praeger Publishers.

McGoldrick, M., & Giordano, J. (1996). Overview: Ethnicity and family therapy. In M. McGoldrick, J. K. Pearce, & J. Giordano (Eds.), *Ethnicity & Family Therapy 2nd edition* (pp. 3-30), New York: The Guilford Press.

Meeks, B. W. (2004). *"Jamaica"*. World Book Online Reference Center. Retrieved 12/30/2005, from http://www.aolsvc.worldbook.aol.com.

Migration Policy Institute. Retrieved 08/11/2023, from https://www.migrationpolicy.org/article
Article: Caribbean Immigrants in the United States | migrationpolicy.org

Murrell, N. S. *Jamaican Americans. Countries and their cultures.* Retrieved 08/11/2023, from http://www.everyculture.com/multi/Ha-La/Jamaican- Americans.html#ixzz17cUR2lXn

Segal, A. (1987). The Caribbean exodus in a global context: Comparative migration experiences. In B. B. Levine (Ed.), The Caribbean Exodus (pp. 15-31). New York: Praeger Publishers.

Segal, R. (1995). *The black diaspora.* New York: Farrar, Straus & Giroux.

Utsey, S. O., Chae, M. H., Brown, C. F., & Kelly, D. (2002). Effect of ethnic group membership on ethnic identity, race-related stress, and quality of life. *Cultural Diversity and Ethnic Minority Psychology 8* (4), 366-377.

Waters, M. C. (1994). Ethnic and racial identities of second-generation Black immigrants in New York City. *International migration Review, 28* (4), 795-818.

Worthy, L. D., Lavigne, T., & Romero, F. (2022). Berry's model of acculturation. Maricopa Open Digital Press. https://open.maricopa.edu/culturepsychology.

Milton Keynes UK
Ingram Content Group UK Ltd.
UKHW021619050624
443649UK00016BA/916